- Successful Dating -

No More Frogs
Leo

23 July – 22 August

by
Cathrine Dahl

CONTENTS

- Successful Dating -
No More Frogs

by Cathrine Dahl

No More Frogs - Successful Dating is your one-stop dating guide. No unnecessary blah-blah. The information is right here, at your fingertips.

This guide can be used in several ways. It's a handy tool when you want to prepare yourself a little. It can give you an advantage when going on a date or getting to know someone you've just met - or even someone you've known for a while.

Although this guide can help you angle your approach, remember to be true to yourself. Have fun, be wise, follow your heart - and keep your feet on the ground!

- Cathrine Dahl

Preface:
A few words about compatibility, and why compatibility guides can give you the wrong idea.

So you've met this Gemini you really, really like, but you're a Scorpio, and the compatibility guides say you're a lousy match. Guess what? That's rubbish!

Some compatibility guides offer a very simplistic approach, claiming that your best matches are the star signs within the same element as you:

Fire: Aries, Leo and Sagittarius
Earth: Taurus, Virgo and Capricorn
Air: Gemini, Libra and Aquarius
Water: Cancer, Scorpio and Pisces

Other guides are slightly more specific, declaring that we are compatible with star signs within our astrological polarity.

Yin: Taurus, Virgo, Capricorn, Cancer, Scorpio and Pisces
Yang: Aries, Leo, Sagittarius, Gemini, Libra and Aquarius

Doesn't look too good, does it? The most optimistic approach has removed half of the population from your dating pool. It doesn't make any sense. The true picture is far more promising...

One star sign, two very different personalities

Each of us has a unique astrological thumbprint determined by the sun, the moon and the planets. The most important factors being your ascending star (ascendant), the sun (star sign) and the moon (feelings).

Let's make it simple
Imagine your star sign being a melody. All the other aspects (the unique positioning of the moon and the planets) are sound effects, applied by a producer with a mixer.

The combination of rhythm, depth and base creates your unique sound. Another person with the same star sign will get his own sound mix and end up with a different beat.

Your personal melody can create wonderful harmonies with star signs you're not supposed to get on with – and nothing but noise with signs that are meant to be matches. You won't find out until you get to know each other.

Let's get to know your date...

THE MALE

YOUR DATE: LEO
23 July–22 August

The Essence of him

Impossible to ignore – confident – generous – social – enthusiastic – positive – big-hearted – has a big personality – energetic and lively – engaging – encouraging – masculine – boyish – playful – loves being the centre of attention – loyal – reliable – flashy – careless with money – attentive – kind – agreeable – friendly – understanding – superficial – temperamental – naturally authoritative

...and remember: Don't forget to show your interest in him by asking questions and expressing admiration for who he is and what he's done.

Blind Date – speedy essentials

Who's waiting for you?

Forget about shy and modest guys with sweaty palms and nervous glances. This guy will leap up from his chair and greet you with a charismatic smile. He will look you in the eye and not be afraid to establish physical contact with you right away. He will be genuinely pleased to see you. The Leo man radiates enthusiasm, and it may almost seem like his entire body is smiling. If the first impression is right and the two of you click, then you're in for a very exciting evening – and his body language will give this away. All said, this is a man who is capable of sweeping you off your feet in minutes.

Emergency fixes for embarrassing pauses

A quiet Leo? He must be suffering from the flu with a high fever. Being quiet is against his nature. He is outgoing and enthusiastic, and embarrassing pauses simply do not exist in his world – or at least, they're extremely rare. Although talking and socialising come easily to him, he won't mind you taking the initiative. Just make sure to be positive. Avoid bringing up bad news.

Your place or mine?

If you ask a Leo, life is for living, loving – and lusting. Why wait until later? If the two of you hit it off and feel the erotic temperature rising, then he won't need much encouragement to take the next step. The more he likes you, the better the chance that he'll suggest a coffee at his place – or yours. This guy has no inhibitions.

Checklist, before you dash out to meet him:

Be on time

(hint: Don't be stressed)

Wear modest, feminine make-up

(hint: Not too much. Keep it classy)

Rinse your mouth and floss your teeth

(hint: Flash a beautiful and fresh smile)

Wear a designer item or something a little luxurious

(hint: He enjoys the finer things in life)

Brush up on positive news

(hint: Keep an optimistic approach)

Tip: If he really likes you, he will pamper you. Never undercut his generosity with comments like: 'That's too much' or 'That's too expensive'. Be happy. Be positive. Be grateful!

CHAPTER 1

PREPARE YOURSELF

Catch his eye, capture his attention
Top 10 attention grabbers

1. Allow yourself to be admired by men, and respond with a smile.
2. Be stylish and show off a hint of luxury.
3. Carry yourself with femininity and grace.
4. Flatter him in public.
5. Let him know you admire him.
6. Put a positive spin on everything.
7. Be sparkling and happy – and show off a genuine smile.
8. Take the initiative to suggest something fun or unusual to do.
9. Wear something expensive.
10. Impress him with something you've done, but don't outshine him.

The SHE. The woman!

He needs a woman who can shine by his side – a jewel to make him look good. In return, he will treat her like a queen. She must be stylish, attractive and feminine, and know a little about a lot of things. He wants someone smart, but she doesn't need to have a doctorate; although he is confident, he can actually feel uncomfortable in the company of a woman he suspects is smarter than he is. His ideal woman must appreciate his masculinity and express her affection clearly. Praising and flattering him is also very important.

The Essence of her

Stylish – attractive – feminine – entertaining – smart, without being too intellectual – up-to-date on current affairs – attentive – has a positive outlook – generous – enjoys the pleasures of life – supportive and loyal - adventurous and playful – sensual, with a fondness for sex – vocal in her admiration- productive and constructive

Leo arousal meter

From 0 to 100... In less than 10 minutes – or it could be a week. It depends on the encouragement he gets. The good thing is, it's up to you…

Remember: Be true to yourself

It doesn't matter if he is the most stunning guy you've ever met – if you don't match, you don't match. You may be able to put on a show for a while to hold his attention, but what's the point? We can't please everybody. We all have different needs, dreams, tastes and preferences. There's no such thing as a one-size-fits-all lover. Be yourself, and be true to who you are – always!

Very important: Be charming and outgoing, but never steal his spotlight. If he feels like he is standing in your shadow, it won't take him long to head off to find a place where he can shine.

CHAPTER 2

THE FIRST DATE

Getting your foot in the door
The basics

You don't have to be a model... but make sure you look good. Emphasise your feminine features.

Be interesting. Let him know that you have a fondness for everything new and exciting – without coming across as a trend-follower.

Flatter him. Look into his eyes and tell him he's the best-looking guy you've met in a long time. This won't scare him off. He'll love the praise.

Look at the bright side. Humour is important if you want to capture him. Make him laugh and focus on the sunny sides of life.

Be generous. After you've seen him a couple of times, buy him a gift. Make sure it has luxury written all over it. It doesn't have to be big – just let him know you appreciate nice things.

A little competition... Let him see you surrounded by attentive males. This strategy never fails. Mr Leo is eager to capture a woman who is popular with other men.

Whatever you do...

• **DON'T** boss him around.

• **DON'T** try to outsmart him or point out his mistakes.

• **DON'T** talk about ex-boyfriends.

• **DON'T** wear anything too suggestive.

• **DON'T** make jokes on his behalf, even innocent ones.

Remember,
There's no need to feel shy about his generosity. If he really likes you, he will love

• **DON'T** suggest that something he bought for you might be

too expensive.

• **DON'T** be negative.

• **DON'T** suggest splitting the bill.

• **DON'T** agree with him just for the sake of it.

• **DON'T** play games or tease him, no matter how innocently.

spoiling you. Just remember
to let him know how grateful
you are.

Signs you're in - or not

If a Leo man likes you, you'll know! He's simple in this regard: either he likes you or he doesn't. He doesn't need to think about it forever. If it feels right, he'll go for it. If it's not working out, he'll deal with it. Either way, he won't waste time. If he's into you, there will be no evasive hints or modest gifts. He won't give you a single rose. He'll give you a dozen. He won't just invite you out for pizza; he'll dance with you under the stars. Still not sure? Here are some ways to tell that Mr Leo is smitten:

Chances are he will...

- give you a gift or a little surprise
- pop by – not to check on you, but just to say hi
- show you off to his friends
- call to make sure you made it home safely
- suggest going away together
- show genuine interest in what you're up to

Not your type? Making an exit

This man will never stay in a relationship with a woman who has turned into a grey cloud over his life. He needs happiness and positivity to grow and flourish, and he can't do this without optimism and energy. He wants a partner who shines and makes the days happy and bright. If you fail to meet his expectations, chances are he'll be the one getting rid of you. He loves women. This is a popular guy, and he won't have any trouble moving on.

If you are getting tired of the whole thing, but Mr Leo is still around, you've obviously managed to charm him deeply. He probably sees a side to you that he finds exciting. Or maybe you're a jewel he likes to show off out in public. In that case, it's time to show him your less-appealing side...

Foolproof exit measures:

If you go ahead with these suggestions, you will come across as mean, cynical and cold. There will be no turning back from this.

- Criticise his spending, even if he has spent the money on you
- Accuse him of living in a fantasy world
- Never offer any praise or approval
- Let yourself go. Be indifferent about your looks
- Interrupt him and argue with him constantly – in public as well
- Tell him to stop being so childish and to behave like a man

CHAPTER 3

SEX'N STUFF

Seductive moves:
How to get him in the mood:

Admiring his body is a good start. Don't forget his 'toolbox'. He's very proud of his equipment, regardless of size. If you show sensual admiration while the two of you are out on the town, he will probably turn into a wonderful and passionate stud as soon as you are back home.

Preferences and erotic nature

Remember to let him know how much you enjoy ... well, everything: him, his body, his lovemaking – the lot. Don't leave it until later. Show your pleasure in bed with words, sighs and touches. This will fuel his passion and keep him going. He's not an adventurous lover, and he's happy with traditional stuff. Never criticise him or ask him to change his ways. If you want to try something new, present it as an exciting suggestion. Don't push him if he doesn't seem eager. When the time has come to sleep, never turn your back on him. Take time to cuddle and praise him. If you forget to do this, he will probably start sulking.

Hitting the right buttons

Although every sign has areas on the body that are more sensitive than others, individual sensitivity may vary quite a bit. Don't go body-blind. Honing in on these erogenous zones and forgetting the rest of him is not a good idea. Use these areas to create sparks while turning him on, and as a passion-booster when things get heated. Watch his body language – including the most obvious of signs. Open your mind to the sensuality of touch and taste.

Key area
His back

Get it on
If you give him an innocent back massage, you could be in for a passionate response. The lighter the touch, the heavier the breathing. If you're not in the mood for sex, make sure the pressure is firm.

Arouse him
Be gentle. Let the tips of your fingers gently play over his bare back. Soft lips and a playful tongue will make his heart beat faster. Rubbing his back with a towel as he gets out of the shower will usually evolve into something more passionate. When out in public, there are endless ways to arouse him without drawing attention. An innocent hug could turn into a very intimate and sensual moment – and be a good reason to quickly hail a taxi back home.

Surprise him

Give him a flirtatious call during the day. There's no need to be blunt; he's got a pretty good imagination. Suggest meeting up later that evening...

Spice it up

The 'helpless female' act is a great turn-on for this guy, as it gives him a chance to show off his masculine side. Oh, and sassy feminine underwear is a plus.

Remember: Never, ever, give the impression that you're up for an erotic encounter just to measure his interest. This can cause him to lose trust in you, and change the way he feels about you.

His expectations

Hot'n spicy. Sex is an important part of his life. He takes passion seriously.

No mixed signals. Avoid playful teasing. Other guys may be turned on by it. This guy will be offended.

Be vocal. Verbal affirmations turn him on, both inside and outside the bedroom. He loves, and needs, to be stimulated with words. A woman who tells him how much she admires him as a lover and praises his body – and how he uses it – will always have a special place in his heart.

No lazy chicks! He needs a woman who is active in bed. A passive partner can shift his mood from steamy to chilly in no time.

A little bit of everything. His ideal partner will be feminine, playful and passionate.

Your sensual preferences
Quiz yourself and find out whether this man is for you.

Where on the scale are you?
1 = Don't agree | 3 = Sure | 5 = Agree!

1. Hot and exciting sex requires a man to be passionate and dominant in bed.
One a scale for 1 to 5, you are : 1 - 2 - 3- 4 - 5

2. Expressing pleasure during sex is very important.
One a scale for 1 to 5, you are : 1 - 2 - 3- 4 - 5

3. There is no need for drawn-out foreplay in order to experience passion and pleasure.
One a scale for 1 to 5, you are : 1 - 2 - 3- 4 - 5

4. Passion and erotic impulsiveness are far more important than gadgets and new positions.
One a scale for 1 to 5, you are : 1 - 2 - 3- 4 - 5

Score 15–20: You have the capacity to thoroughly enjoy exploring each other passionately – and frequently.
Score 10–14: There will be loads of passion and very few slow moments. Just remember to convey your feelings of pleasure clearly.
Score 5–9: As long as you give him the encouragement he needs, both verbally and physically, he will do his best to please you.
Score 1–4: This guy may be a little too passionate and direct for you at times. Don't tell him to slow down while you're in the middle of things. Tell him about your preferences before having sex. If you do it seductively, he will remember.

CHAPTER 4

GENERAL STUFF

The big picture

Keep in mind that the characteristics of a Leo may vary quite a bit depending on where within the sign he was born, as well as a wide range of additional astrological factors. But for now, let's stick to the basics. Just remember: don't jump to conclusions as soon as you meet him. Give him room to shine. Get to know the man behind the sign.

His personality: Pros and cons

Pros	Cons
• Generous	• Childish
• Has a positive outlook on life	• Careless with money
• Enthusiastic	• Blunt
• Confident	• Temperamental
• Lives in the moment	• Stubborn
• Has a big personality	• Ambitious, even ruthless
• Masculine	• Selfish
• Playful and boyish	• Demanding of attention
• Encouraging	• Impressed by status and wealth
• Entertaining	• Easily offended
• Loyal	• Takes himself too seriously
• Honest	• Unable to tolerate criticism
• Trustworthy	• Self-centered
• Stylish	• Snobbish

Tip: How to show romantic interest

Express admiration and treat him to little luxuries, like a special wine or a beer, cashmere socks, etc. Make sure he knows you've made an effort.

Romantic Vibes

Mr Leo:
The protective and generous partner

The essence

Royal treatment. The Leo man will pamper and spoil his woman in every way. He will treat her like a like a queen. There is only one small catch ... she must accept him as the king.

Embrace his manliness. A woman who can handle his masculinity will reap the rewards of his generosity and attentiveness.

My woman! He loves showing off an attractive partner, but he doesn't like competition and can become jealous if you receive too much attention from other guys when you're out. The same applies to male friends and former boyfriends.

Reliable. He is very loyal and will come rushing whenever you need help or guidance.

Genuinely positive and optimistic. Although he may seem to have everything under control, some Leos are just keeping their fingers crossed and hoping for the best. This has nothing to do with laziness; he just genuinely believes that everything will be fine. But you don't need to worry. He has a unique gift of landing on his feet.

Tip: How to show erotic interest

Whisper erotic suggestions into his ear, but don't be crude about it. Emphasise his strength and qualities as a lover, and tell him how much you are looking forward to feeling him...

Erotic Vibrations

Mr Leo:
The powerful and positive lover

The essence

Enthusiasm. It's impossible to be indifferent about sex while dating a Leo. He is just as enthusiastic about sex as he is about everything else in life, and it's infectious. If your ideal lover is quiet, gentle and sensitive, you may find him a little overwhelming.

Don't hold back. Passion is his middle name, and he expects his partner to be just as excited. But don't worry – he won't turn sex into an exhausting marathon. He knows when he needs to take it easy.

Great lover. A Leo takes great pride in pleasing his partner, and he seldom fails. One hint is all it takes, and he'll be ready to prove himself as the world's greatest lover.

Knows his way around. There will be no insecure fumbling under the covers. This guy knows what he's doing, and he's usually pretty good at it. He is straight to the point and can go for hours without getting bored or tired.

No games! Whatever you do, never tease him. This guy doesn't enjoy playing games! If you have accepted an intimate invitation from him, you'd better finish what you started.

When he's hot, he's hot. This guy doesn't waste time. He will probably sweep you off your feet sooner than you think...

CHAPTER 5

COMPATIBILITY QUIZ

Are you banging your head against the wall, or does he unleash your positive potential? Do you provoke him or bring out the best in him? Does he make you throw your arms up in exasperation, or do you feel inspired and complete in his company? Are the two of you headed towards doom or dream? Take the test to find out.

Question 1.
Your man enthusiastically tells you about an project he's about to start working on. What's your reaction?

A. I'd say, 'Wow, great!' I don't want to ruin his enthusiasm, even though I know he tends to lose interest if things don't meet his expectations.
B. I'd probably ask him if he had given it enough thought. I've heard the same story many times before.
C. I'd share his enthusiasm – of course. I love positive men!

Question 2.
You've just finished a romantic dinner when he looks at you passionately and says: 'Come and join me in the jungle!' How do you respond?

A. With excitement.
B. I'd quite like that – even though his erotic invitations can be a little unrefined at times...
C. Sigh. I'm so tired of his macho stuff. I'd have told him to help me clear the table instead

(cont.)

Question 3.
Do you think it's OK for you partner to try and impress other women?

A. No, not at all. Whenever he tries to convince the world that he's Mr Wonderful, I feel completely ignored.
B. It's no problem for me. He is who he is, and I'm proud of him.
C. It's OK, provided he doesn't overdo it.

Question 4.
Do you get nervous when your checking account balance gets low?

A. It depends how many bills I have lying around.
B. Of course! I don't print new money in the kitchen.
C. I'm pretty relaxed about it. If I have spent a little too much one month, I'll save a little extra the next.

Question 5.
Have you ever cuddled up with your man, aroused him ... and then rolled over to sleep?

A. Never! That's mean and insensitive!
B. I did once, for fun ... but he didn't like that.
C. Sure. I love teasing my partner.

Question 6.
How do you deal with your partner if he suddenly gets quiet and withdraws into himself?

A. Everyone needs a little space sometimes. I leave him alone and make sure he knows I'm there if he needs me.
B. Nothing much. He can get a little grumpy, but I don't know why he always has to take it out on me.
C. There's only one thing to do: I am sweet and gentle to him.

Question 7.
Do you express pleasure clearly when having sex?

A. Not really; I'm not all that passionate.
B. Absolutely. It's impossible not to – my partner is hot.
C. Depends on my mood. Sometimes I like to take it slow and easy.

Question 8.
How would you define excitement?

A. Streaming an action movie.
B. Everyday surprises, sensuality and love.
C. Days without routine, a spontaneous sex life, travel and new experiences – big and small.

Question 9.
Do you think it's important to flatter your partner's body in bed?

A. Sometimes, but only if it feels natural to do so.
B. Yes, absolutely – both with words and touches.
C. I've never really thought about it.

Question 10.
How do you feel about sex that is intensely passionate from the very first second?

A. It's wonderful – once in a while.
B. I love it. Passion makes me feel alive.
C. Not my favourite. I'm not into sexual gymnastics.

SCORE	A	B	C
Question 1	10	5	1
Question 2	5	1	10
Question 3	1	10	5
Question 4	5	1	10
Question 5	10	5	1
Question 6	10	1	5
Question 7	1	10	5
Question 8	1	5	10
Question 9	5	10	1
Question 10	5	10	1

75 – 100

The most perfect, attractive and exciting man could walk into your life tomorrow – and you would ignore him. You have already found the man who can transform any rainy day into an exciting adventure. You know how important it is to encourage people around you, including your Leo. You make the sun shine for him, and he rewards you by pampering you in every way possible. Your sexual chemistry is strong, and you are simply hooked on each other. Passion flows naturally and freely ... wow. Full steam ahead!

51 – 74

You understand the importance of compliments: without reassurance and positive input, life can become lethargic and uninspiring. You are the kind of woman who helps this man open up and enjoy life. Remember that the Leo needs to establish himself as the dominating male, but don't let this put you off. He has no urge to control you; he only wants to show you that he's capable of protecting and taking care of you – including in the bedroom. Sex is important to him. Although he may not appreciate that you're not as active as he is, he will respect your honesty and do whatever it takes to please you.

26 – 50

One thing is certain: this relationship will never be boring. In fact, sparks will fly quite frequently – sometimes positive sparks, sometimes negative. Avoid obvious bummers like stepping on his ego. Constructive criticism during sex is another no-no. He has zero tolerance for criticism in bed, and even helpful comments can turn him off completely. Show him love and admiration, and be the queen by his side. Don't deny him the odd moment of luxury from time to time – even though you may not be in the mood for splurging. Too much work? It will probably be trying at times, but if you like him, there aren't many options. He is kind, passionate and generous. He is also self-centered, childish and temperamental. If you feel his negative sides overshadows his positive ones, you may want to explore love elsewhere.

10 – 25

Some relationships are challenging. This one is basically just hard work. It doesn't matter if you mean well, or that you act out of care for him: fussing will get you nowhere. The only thing you'll achieve is putting him in a bad mood – and a miserable Leo is a pain. He feeds on admiration and love. If you deny him this, he will lose his sparkle – and eventually lose himself. He is careful not to let this happen, so if things aren't going well, he will probably be out of your life before you get a chance to kick him out. Happiness waits elsewhere – for both of you.

Thoughts...
Time, effort and love will determine whether this relationship is built to last. Embrace everything that feels good, and be constructive about the rest.

THE FEMALE

YOUR DATE: LEO
23 July–22 August

The Essence of her

Confident – determined – optimistic–enthusiastic, with a flair for drama – assertive and strong – temperamental – generous – restless – attractive and particular about her looks – motivational and inspirational, both privately and at work – sensual and passionate – assertive – sets high standards for herself and others

...and remember: Although she will probably approach you with friendly enthusiasm, it's up to you to hold her interest. She is genuine about everything and won't stick around just to be polite.

Blind Date – speedy essentials

Who's waiting for you?

She won't be waiting for you! This queen doesn't sit around waiting for a guy – unless he has called and told her that he'll be late, has a very good excuse and has ordered a bottle of champagne to her table. Otherwise, you'll need to be there early, waiting for her. You'll notice her immediately. She doesn't walk through a door; she makes an entrance. There's something about her that makes people look. She's graceful and sensual, and she moves with confidence. Her beauty radiates from within. She will greet you with a cheerful smile and devastating eye contact.

Emergency fixes for embarrassing pauses.

Although she's naturally bubbly, confident and outgoing, the conversation may need a slight boost before you're completely comfortable in each other's company – or if she's so dazzled by your charm and personality that she's speechless. Compliment her for something you can talk more about. Voice: Are you a singer? Movement: Are you into dancing? Get creative about it.

Your place or mine?

Preferably a luxurious hotel room... The Leo woman loves adventure and excitement. If you're handsome, attentive, charming and generous, then she may be open to an erotic encounter. She believes that life is for living, and she is no prude. But this doesn't mean she'll accept any erotic invitation. She is choosy, and her standards are high. However, the right man may just persuade her to share a few sensual pleasures...

Checklist, before you dash out to meet her:

Have a small surprise arranged: Champagne at the table,
for example (hint: Be generous)

Wear clothing that emphasises your best features
(hint: Avoid being too obvious)

Be up-to-date on the social scene
(hint: Suggestions going to a show or an exhibition)

Scan the news for positive stories ahead of time
(hint: No negative vibes)

Be perfectly groomed with a slight hint of cologne
(hint: Be attractive and masculine)

Tip: In her world, there can never be too much of a good thing. The more, the better. This applies to everything, from praise and sensual attention to adventure and luxury.

CHAPTER 1

PREPARE YOURSELF

Catch her eye, capture her attention
Top 10 attention grabbers

1. No matter what looks you were born with, be stunning – it's all about confidence.
2. Surprise her with something unusual.
3. Be generous but don't be a show-off.
4. Be humorous and make her laugh.
5. Approach everyday topics from a positive and constructive angle.
6. Be classy and stylish. Pay careful attention to your attire.
7. Got an expensive car or luxury item? Make sure she sees it.
8. Take her to a place where people know you and give you little extras.
9. Share something interesting you know about music, food or drink.
10. Carry yourself with style and be someone she feels proud of being seen with.

The HE. The man!

Although the Leo woman is a great flirt, she won't chase a man. She will simply draw attention to herself and wait for him to make a move. However, if he waits too long, she may already be off. Her ideal man is confident, masculine and able to sweep her off her feet. He will be attentive, handsome and generous. It's important that he gives her room to shine – and never makes her stand in his shadow!

The Essence of him
Stylish and distinguished – gallant – generous with money, affection and praise – handsome – successful, in one way or another – attentive – strong – courageous – passionate and erotic – has a flair for luxury and comfort – confident and charming around women, but never flirtatious and always loyal – physically active and fit

Leo arousal meter
From 0 to 100... In an hour – or a week. It depends on her partner. She can't be bothered to spend time on someone who fails to inspire and excite her.

Remember: Be true to yourself

It doesn't matter if she is the most stunning girl you've ever met – if you don't match, you don't match. You may be able to put on a show for a while to hold her attention, but what's the point? We can't please everybody. We all have different needs, dreams, tastes and preferences. There's no such thing as a one-size-fits-all lover. Be yourself, and be true to who you are – always!

Very important: Never compete with her for a space in the spotlight. Allow her to take centre stage, and be proud of her.

CHAPTER 2

THE FIRST DATE

Getting your foot in the door
The basics

Admiration is king. You will get absolutely nowhere without praise and admiration. But this won't be a problem. As soon as you meet her, you'll find yourself paying her one compliment after another without even thinking about it.

In demand. Prepare yourself for competition. This sparkling and glamorous woman has many admirers. If you want to win her over, you'd better be attentive.

Keep it positive. Don't expect her to take on your problems. She's not all that keen on problems. Her attitude toward life is optimistic, and problems rarely exist in her world – she sees challenges as temporarily setbacks. Pessimistic or over-burdened guys won't stand a chance.

Roll out the red carpet. She loves to be where the action is, so it might be a good idea to take her to a new club, a premiere at the theatre or even on a weekend abroad.

Splash out. Don't invite her out to just any old restaurant. Make it somewhere special or exclusive. Being extravagant is fine. In fact, the Leo woman will love it.

Whatever you do...

- **DON'T** flirt with other women.

- **DON'T** forget to call or text her.

- **DON'T** bother her with worries and problems.

- **DON'T** be a cheapskate.

- **DON'T** make her have to work to earn your admiration.

Remember,
Never keep her waiting. If she has shown interest in you, she expects to hear from you right away. If it seems like you're dragging your feet,

- **DON'T** ask her to split the restaurant bill or suggest she

pay the tip.

- **DON'T** criticise her – not even constructive criticism.

- **DON'T** patronise her.

- **DON'T** bargain with the waiter to get a free dessert.

- **DON'T** demand her attention and talk about yourself.

she'll probably decide that you're not her type after all and move on to one of the more energetic and attentive guys on her list.

Signs you're in - or not

The Leo woman prefers being chased. But this doesn't mean she won't make an effort to show interest. If she likes you, she will let you know – and subtle hints are not her style. Her motto is 'If you want something, go for it!' The man who has managed to capture her interest will represent a challenge and an adventure for her. If she hasn't made it obvious already, these behaviours will indicate that she sees you more than a just a fling:

Chances are she will...

- show you off to her friends
- let you steal her spotlight
- treat you to something nice, like a gift or a meal
- act seductive and erotically assertive
- take the initiative to ask you out
- she will send you flirtatious texts

Not your type? Making an exit

The Leo woman loves life. She loves men. She loves attention, admiration and desire. It's very unlikely that she'll ever be stuck in a joyless relationship. She is not some feeble woman who needs a strong man by her side. She embraces every day with enthusiasm and joy. If you find yourself stuck in a relationship with a Leo, then you really must be a stunner! There must be a very special reason why she's not prepared to let go.

You won't really have to make an effort to break it off. A simple comment like 'You're pretty good in bed, but you need to kick it up a notch in order to make it onto my "top ten lovers" list' will cause her to freak out. She may lose her temper, but she won't get emotional. She's not prepared to waste emotional energy on a man she regards as a jerk.

Foolproof exit measures:

If you want to make absolutely sure that your parting-ways message gets through, try the following:

- Criticise her hot passion in bed
- Tell her to lose weight and exercise more
- Flirt with other women when you're out together
- Insist on taking control in bed – and get it over with pretty quickly
- Surprise her with a weekend away – at a cheap motel in a neighbouring town
- Focus on yourself: your looks, your job, your future

CHAPTER 3

SEX'N STUFF

Seductive moves:
How to get her in the mood:

A Leo lady wants a masculine man. She wants a guy who knows what he's doing and where he's going. Boyish playfulness can be fun, but it's not what she's after in the long run. Assertiveness is the driving force of her life, and she brings it into the bedroom as well. Her partner needs to be strong enough to appreciate her passion and even take it a bit further.

Preferences and erotic nature

She is not shy. She loves physical attention on every inch of her body. The tip of your tongue, soft and relaxed lips, the tips of your fingers ... use your imagination. Take your time. Don't confine yourself to her neck and chest; move all the way from her toes up to her thighs and tummy, and she will wriggle with pleasure. She loves showing off her body, both in bed and turning you on before you get there. Role-play can be very arousing for her – she'd enjoy meeting a strong man who reluctantly allows her to dominate him, or a more sexually insecure man who needs a confident partner.

Hitting the right buttons

Although every sign has areas on the body that are more sensitive than others, individual sensitivity may vary quite a bit. Don't go body-blind. Honing in on these erogenous zones and forgetting the rest of her is not a good idea. Use these areas to create sparks while turning her on, and as a passion-booster when things get heated. Watch her body language – including the most obvious of signs. Open your mind to the sensuality of touch and taste.

Key area
Her back

Get it on
'Are you tired, babe? Let me give you a backrub.' A slightly dated and worn-out suggestion, perhaps? It may be, but it still works well with the female Leo if you want to create a few sparks.

Arouse her
Every gentle touch to a Leo's back sends sensual signals to her brain. Your hands are not the only tools you can use to stimulate her. Try your lips, tongue and other body parts. Increase the intensity as you go along, but don't start off too rough. Pay attention to her back when you're out in public as well. Soft caresses will make her burst with anticipation...

Surprise her

Initiate sex when she least expects it. Invite her home for a long lunch – and don't tell her that it could be a very erotic lunch. Make sure to pick the right day. The interlude won't be a success if she's got deadlines or a meeting to prepare for.

Spice it up

Ask her to strip for you. Get the music going and get comfortable. Make sure to get into it – not just excited, but also vocal and suggestive. Fire her up.

Remember: Her enjoyment of taking the initiative doesn't mean you can just lie back and enjoy it all. She wants a passionate and active lover, not merely a toolbox to fiddle around with.

Her expectations

No quickies. The setting needs to be right. If you're hoping for quick one in the backseat of your car, you will be disappointed.

Know your stuff. The Leo woman enjoys being sexually assertive, but she also doesn't mind a dominating partner – provided he knows how to please her.

Body talk. Admiration plays an important role in her erotic life. She prefers to make love with the lights on, and the reason is obvious: She wants her partner to admire her body. She may even rub herself with oil during foreplay in order to make her body appear sexier.

Take your time. Don't rush her. Never move on from one thing to the next too quickly. This will annoy her. She loves taking her time and enjoying every sensation.

Exposure. She prefers positions that allow her to expose her body as much as possible, so her partner has ample opportunity to caress her and tell her how wonderful she looks.

Getting pampered. If you're tired or don't feel particularly inspired, she will gladly run the show – as long as you admire her and respond with passion.

Your sensual preferences
Quiz yourself and find out whether this woman is for you.

Where on the scale are you?
1 = Don't agree | 3 = Sure | 5 = Agree!

1. Expressiveness is liberating, and it's important for fully enjoying sex.
One a scale for 1 to 5, you are: 1 - 2 - 3- 4 - 5

2. An assertive and passionate lover is very arousing.
One a scale for 1 to 5, you are: 1 - 2 - 3- 4 - 5

3. During sex, being able to watch is almost as important as being able to touch
One a scale for 1 to 5, you are: 1 - 2 - 3- 4 - 5

4. There's no such thing as sex without passion.
One a scale for 1 to 5, you are: 1 - 2 - 3- 4 - 5

Score.
15 - 20: There's only one thing to say: Close the windows and enjoy!
10 - 14: Her passionate side may surprise you, but she won't disappoint you – far from it. She may even open a few doors to new erotic adventures.
05 - 09: Don't be put off by her assertiveness. Allow yourself to relax and let her guide the way. Settle into the erotic feelings and notice how the passion builds.
01 - 04: She might be a bit too much to handle at times. Communicate is very important. She is no mind reader.

CHAPTER 4

GENERAL STUFF

The big picture

Keep in mind that the characteristics of a Leo may vary quite
a bit depending on where within the sign she was born, as
well as a wide range of additional astrological factors. But for
now, let's stick to the basics. Just remember: don't jump to
conclusions as soon as you meet her. Give her room to shine.
Get to know the woman behind the sign.

Her personality: Pros and cons

Pros	Cons
• Positive	• Self-centered
• Generous	• Superficial
• Passionate	• Temperamental
• Optimistic and cheerful	• Jealous
• Spontaneous and exciting	• Hides from difficulties
• Affectionate and loyal	• Thoughtless
• Confident	• Ruthless
• Has a strong personality	• Spoiled
• Attractive	• Vain
• Sensual and erotic	• Easily bored
• Assertive	• A drama queen
• Motivating	• Hyperactive
• Genuine	• Reckless
• Courageous	• Suppresses disappointments

Tip: How to show romantic interest

Don't hold back – on anything!
Shower her with attention, but
without being pushy. Pamper her
with invitations and little gifts. A
note on flowers: Avoid the selection
at your local petrol station. Make it
classy and special.

Romantic Vibes

Miss Leo:
The intense and enthusiastic partner

The essence

Keep her interested. She falls in and out of love frequently, and it takes a very special man to capture her heart.

Be attentive. Affection, attention and loads of praise are important for keeping her interest alive.

Don't get too comfortable. Never take her love for granted. A miserable Leo won't stay miserable for long, and she'll go find a more attentive male.

Telling you straight. She has a fierce temper and won't hesitate to tell you how she feels if you have upset her.

Excitement is important. This applies to her romantic life as well. She will never allow love to become a chore or even a routine. She sees love as a living thing, and she will nourish it.

Seize the moment. She doesn't get sentimental. She prefers to live her life and not spend in brooding over the past. Ex-boyfriends are ex-boyfriends.

It takes two! Although she's a warm and supportive partner, she expects her man to do his part in order to make the relationship happy and fulfilling.

Tip: How to show erotic interest

Compliment her curves, the way she moves and the sensuality that exudes from her. Tell her that she really excites you. She adores attentive men.

Erotic Vibrations

Miss Leo:
The assertive and passionate lover

The essence

Privileged.   Self-confidence is her middle name, and you will seldom hear her thanking her lucky stars for providing her with such a wonderful lover. In her opinion, it's he who should be grateful!

Attractive. She never works very hard to capture a man, simply because she doesn't have to. Men are captivated by her positive attitude.

Wonderful. Although slightly self-centered, she is a fantastic lover. She can be very passionate and expressive when things get steamy.

Loosen up. A slightly reserved partner doesn't need to worry. Passionate sex with a Leo woman is usually enough to make him lose his inhibition.

Royal treatment. Her attitude about sex is very relaxed, which is part of the reason why so many men find her irresistible. She will never give her partner performance anxiety. The way she arouses him will make him feel like a king and inspire him to do his best to please her.

Make an effort. She expects her lover to make an effort in every way: he must please her physically and mentally, as well as try to look good and emphasise his masculinity.

CHAPTER 5

COMPATIBILITY QUIZ

Are you banging your head against the wall, or does she unleash your positive potential? Do you provoke her or bring out the best in her? Is she making you throw your arms into the air in exasperation, or do you feel inspired and complete in her company? Take the test to find out.

Question 1.
How would you respond if your partner told you about her previous erotic experiences?

A. Smile seductively and suggest jumping into bed...
B. I'd feel excited, but also a little worried about not living up to her expectations.
C. I'd take it with a grain of salt. Some women are all talk.

Question 2.
In a relationship, do you often flatter your partner's body?

A. Yes, whenever she deserves it.
B. Very seldom. Flattery can make a woman conceited.
C. Yes, of course I do. Everybody enjoys a bit of praise.

(cont.)

Question 3.
As soon as you arrive at a party, your partner takes centre stage and dazzles everyone in the room. How do you feel about that?

A. It's typical, and it embarrasses me.
B. I love the positive attention she attracts to herself.
C. It's OK, provided she doesn't overdo it.

Question 4.
How would you feel about a woman who has very high expectations of her partner as a lover?

A. It sounds like a fun challenge.
B. I don't really know. I wouldn't want to feel obliged to perform in a certain way.
C. Well, if that was the case, then I'd better not disappoint her.

Question 5.
What would you do if your girlfriend became overly enthusiastic about all of her ideas?

A. I would support her and make sure she kept in touch with reality.
B. I'd ask her to think about things a little more – even though she hates it when I try to temper her enthusiasm.
C. Nothing. She never listens anyway.

Question 6.
Do you think it's important to let your partner know during sex that you are happy with her as a lover?

A. Of course it is. I tell her all the time.
B. When I'm having sex, I'm having sex – why bring conversation into it?
C. Sometimes I do; sometimes I forget.

Question 7.
Do you enjoy an assertive woman who takes the initiative?

A. I don't know about that. Pushy women don't really appeal to me.
B. Yes, I'm quite assertive myself, and I need a strong and independent partner.
C. Sure, that's nice, provided she doesn't insist on running my life.

Question 8.
How important is passion in your life?

A. Passion is overrated. I prefer to take things slow.
B. About average. If you apply passion to everything you do, life can get hectic.
C. Passion is very important to me. It inspires me and drives me onwards.

Question 9.
Do you pay attention to your partner's entire body during sex?

A. No. When I'm aroused, I seldom have time for that.
B. Yes – it heightens the pleasure for both of us.
C. Yes, during foreplay.

Question 10.
How do you feel about spending money and enjoying the good things in life?

A. Pampering and giving little luxuries keep things exciting and pleasant.
B. My mottos are 'The best things in life are free' and 'Always save for a rainy day'.
C. It's important to treat each other to nice things once in a while.

SCORE	A	B	C
Question 1	10	5	1
Question 2	5	1	10
Question 3	1	10	5
Question 4	5	1	10
Question 5	10	5	1
Question 6	10	1	5
Question 7	1	10	5
Question 8	1	5	10
Question 9	1	10	5
Question 10	10	1	5

75 – 100

A fantasy, a fairy tale? Not for you two! This is real – and very rewarding. People may accuse you of draping yourselves in dreams, but you both know that dreaming is important. Dreams inspire you and bring sunshine into your lives. This relationship will be filled with positivity, enthusiasm and a fair bit of passion. Your communication is strong, and you understand each other. This applies to your intimate life as well. You know how to make the most of your sex life – and how to appreciate it. Keep enjoying life and each other!

51 – 74

She may strike you as a little too much at times, but that's probably what you need. She nudges you when you slow down and energises you when days are grey. Indifference to life is not an option for this girl. She finds the positivity in everything. She believes that life should be fun and filled with love, joy, luxury and fun opportunities. It's impossible to be annoyed with her for long. She can always make you smile, and that makes it easy to forgive and forget. Her standards are very high, and this may present a challenge if you're not particular about your appearance. Remember, she needs a man she can be proud of 24 hours a day, not only in social settings. Cherish her, and enjoy the happiness – and passion – she brings to your life.

26 – 50

Either you don't communicate, or you disagree on the most fundamental issues. Try to identify your differences in order to avoid misunderstandings. There are things you need to keep in mind if you're going to make things work: Never, ever, step on her ego. Avoid criticism; guide her and make suggestions instead. Keep yourself well-groomed – including for your intimate moments. A scruffy lover is a turn-off. Do you measure up to her standards? If not, you'd better do something about it quickly – if you want to, that is. Think about it … is she a little too demanding for your tastes? Yes, she's fun and energetic – but is that enough to make you happy?

10 – 25

Stop criticising her. Fuss and negativity will cause her to lose her passion. Face it: if you want her in your life, you'll have to put up with her extravagant and hyper-positive personality. Are you fed up with constant demands for praise? Does money seem to be flying around? Are you secretly longing for a more stable and down to earth partner? If you want to stay in the fast lane, you'll need to speed up. But maybe it's time to take a more scenic route.

Thoughts...
Too much of anything is too much, and it's up to you to draw the line. Keep in mind that your definition might change over time. What's too much energy today, may be perfect tomorrow. Think twice before making a decision.

...just a final note:
This book has not been approved by your date and should be treated accordingly. He or she *may* not agree with the content.